How To Be Successful Your First Year Selling Life Insurance

LAMAR SKIPPER

Table of Contents

Introduction

Unfortunately, too many agents go through the painful process of obtaining their state's license for selling life insurance only to quit without realizing their goal of success, usually in the first year! Whether it's replacing a job, earning additional income, or becoming your own boss so you can control your time, selling life insurance has allowed millions of people to achieve their goals and it can do the same for you!

This quick and easy-to-read guide to success was written for new agents to provide the necessary foundation to build a successful business and veterans to relight their passion and purpose! Read now to find out what you need to know to participate in this amazing business so you can realize your goals…

Dedication

Lamaria & Lamar Jr., you both are a huge part of the reason I decided to sell life insurance to begin with. It inspires me that both of you want to sell life insurance as well so I dedicate this book to you and the success I know you will have! Let this book help you to succeed faster and allow you to achieve the success you desire!

DID YOU MAKE THE RIGHT CHOICE?

Absolutely! Let me be the first to assure you that if you're willing to invest the time, energy, and effort it takes to be a successful professional, Life Insurance sales can and will provide you with a way to fulfill all of your hopes, dreams, and professional aspirations. I personally believe this is the **BEST INDUSTRY OF ALL!** We provide a product that most people don't want to think or talk about, but all of them need!

But if you're anything like me I'd assume you didn't choose this profession, it probably chose YOU! When most of us were kids we didn't grow up dreaming of being a Life Insurance Agent. Most of us had dreams of being a Police Officer, Firefighter,

Lawyer, Doctor, Nurse, Judge, Dentist, Banker & so on—professions thought to be respectable by most Americans and they are! Life Insurance Agents usually don't make that list. Most people don't aspire to being in sales when imagining life in their younger years and NO ONE goes to college to be a salesman (or woman)!

So how did you get here? How did you decide to become a Life Insurance Agent? If you have even made that decision yet! What life events brought you to the decision to take an online or group class, then a state examination to secure a license to sell insurance products?

In all my years in this profession I have yet to meet anyone who chose this profession while in high school and proceeded to become a agent after graduation with this as their lifetime career choice! Why is that? Why does selling life insurance seem to have a negative stigma attached to it in the minds of so many people? Why wasn't it a career choice for most of the successful agents currently in the business to begin with, myself included?

Let me try and answer these questions by telling you the series of events that brought me to this industry at the ripe and ready age of 22! In my early years I had thoughts of being an FBI Agent and a comedian. TV shows like X files & watching standup comedians like Eddie Murphy and Martin Lawrence got my imagination running wild! But as I got older and got my first real job (when I was 13) at a convince store, my thoughts quickly turned to business! The owner of that store owned several businesses & Real Estate as well. Just watching him and seeing how different the life he had was from the life I grew up in was enough for me to decide that I wanted to be a businessman! I would further this desire by becoming an entrepreneur in high school. My definition of an entrepreneur is a person who solves problems for people at a profit. So in high school I sold candy, CDs, Cars and Doctors notes! Yes, you read that correctly; although Doctors notes wasn't such a good idea by the way. But nonetheless I was always drawn to sales! I was always drawn to providing a needed product to someone who wanted it!

While in high school my interest in business also led me to get into Network Marketing. If you're not familiar with Network Marketing, it's a business that you can join as an independent contractor to market a product or service. I loved the system of marketing that it exposed me too and received a lot of sales training, leadership development and personal development training that became invaluable to me in my insurance sales career! I went from one Network Marketing company to another trying to find the next best thing to get me to where I wanted to be financially.

After graduating high school, I entered college with the desire to learn business but no desire to attend my classes! So after my second semester I dropped out! By then I had already purchased my first home and had a good paying job with a cable company. I wanted to do business, not sit in class and learn it from people who didn't have their own, so I started to develop relationships with people who had established businesses! While still doing Network Marketing I started a Real Estate Company with a friend and we began buying properties to Rehab and Rent them out.

It was during this time I was chosen by the industry. I say "chosen" because I had no interest of selling life insurance and the first time I was offered a policy I had no interest in buying one! Most 21 year olds don't! But I knew how important it was because I saw it firsthand! My mom died my senior year in high school from cancer. This event opened my eyes to the need for insurance and the need to be properly informed. She was a homeowner and like most homeowners she had a mortgage on our house. She wanted me and my brothers to get the house if something happened to her and she thought she had a policy to make that happen—and she did. But unfortunately she refinanced our home 3 weeks before she passed which immediately canceled the coverage she had with the previous lender.

When she called to make sure she still had the coverage, they told her she had to get the protection from her new mortgage company because she wasn't with them anymore. Then when she called the new mortgage company to get the coverage and they started asking her the health question she was told she couldn't get the coverage with them because of her cancer. A few weeks later she was gone! No Life Insurance and No Coverage to pay off the mortgage.

Needless to say I found out the importance of what we do early on!

So at 21 it didn't take a lot of persuasion to get me to buy a policy to protect my family! My introduction into the business happened at the perfect time for me! I had just bought my 2nd home and my twins were about a week out of the hospital. I was a new father and looking for something to replace my income and give me the time freedom I greatly desired so I could be a present father to my Boy/Girl twins: Lamar JR & Lamaria!

During their mom's pregnancy I was denied the opportunity to go to her Doctors' appointment to see their first ultrasound by my job and I promised myself that I would never have to ask permission from a job to be there for my kids. So I was looking for a way to keep that promise! And as the saying goes: seek and you shall find! When I purchased my

2nd home, I received a mail offer for information about mortgage protection—a policy designed to pay off the home at death and provide benefits for disability if something should happen to the homeowner. I filled out the form and returned it through the mail and within a few weeks I was contacted by Ryan, a young professional a few years new to the industry. Ryan came out to my home and presented the mortgage protection product to me and my kid's mom! He explained the need and benefits of the product and after an hour or so we agreed it was a good decision and made the purchase. As Ryan was about to leave I asked him whether he made good money doing this and he looked at me and smiled! He then sat back down and talked to me for another hour about Mortgage Protection & Life Insurance Sales.

He talked about the industry, time freedom and the amazing financial potential of working with their agency! Most of what he said didn't resonate with me at the time but a few things did! The first was about his making $50,000 his first year! That really hit home because it was more than I was making at my current job! Second was the time freedom the profession offered! Those two things were enough to sign me up but I wasn't convinced just yet!

You see, being exposed to Network Marketing had showed me a few things about business and myself. I knew I could sell and I was willing to talk to people, which were ingredients necessary to have any kind of success with Network Marketing. But once I went through my warm market (family and friends) the companies I worked with at the time didn't show me a clear way to make sales and grow my business outside my sphere of influence! And that's what sealed the deal for me! Ryan explained that I could sell to my friends and family but I didn't have too!

Their agency had a lead program that I would have access to which would give me access to qualified prospects that had a need for our product—people who had just purchased a home or refinanced a loan! I could get these leads in my area and surrounding areas who returned the form confirming their interest in the product!

Then I would contact them like he had contacted me to sell them a policy! This got me really excited about replacing my current income with a business that allowed me to control my time! This was just what I was looking for and I was sold! Ryan told me what I needed to do in order to gain access to this profession which held the solution to my problems! He explained that I needed to take my state-approved insurance class and pass an examination. The class was a week long and a total of 40 hours, then further down the line, a 150 multiple-choice test that must be passed!

I took the class a few weeks later for 8 hours a day through a whole week. I was off work at the time due to an automobile accident so the timing was perfect! However, over a month went by before I scheduled my exam! Life with two newborn babies was difficult to say the least and sleep wasn't something I got a lot of back then! So about a month after my class had ended I read the entire book again, scheduled my test and passed it my first time! I remember walking out to my car and calling Ryan to give him the good news! He answered the phone and didn't even remember who I was...Lol! I later found out that I was one of the only people in their agency who had did this on their own. You see I hadn't talked to Ryan since he left my house that night! He told me what I needed to do and I did it and that wasn't common in our industry as he later explained!

I believe our industry doesn't get the recognition it deserves; first because it has such a low cost of entry! Think about it, most professions take years of college and on-job training before you can even call yourself a Lawyer, Doctor, Dentist, Therapist, and on and on. But you can literally take a 40-hour class and pass a state-approved multiple-choice test and voila you can call yourself an *Insurance Agent*! No wonder most people don't take our profession as serious as some of the other professions thought to be more respectable! But let me assure you; we are! We have the same opportunity to earn as much as they do with one extra key benefit—we can control our time and in my opinion that's worth more than the money.

Throughout the rest of this book I will be explaining the ups and downs of my career in this industry, but for now hopefully you can see through my story so far that YOU were chosen by this industry! What events led you here? What thoughts have you had about needs in your life that this industry has the potential to solve? How can working as a Life Insurance Agent allow you to achieve all your goals, dreams and professional aspirations?

The answer to these questions will allow you to get the most out of this industry by giving it the Best You! In the next chapter we will discuss how your mindset can affect your results so let's continue...

CHANGE YOUR MINDSET TO CHANGE YOUR RESULTS

Selling life insurance successfully will require you to have an ownership mindset! If you're coming out of a job and this is your first commission-paid sales position, you may have to change and develop a new mindset that will produce results! So what's your mindset? Is it a job mentality or one of ownership? Let's take a moment and look at the job mentality versus the ownership mentality and how to change your mindset if need be!

The mindset of the job mentality looks on the outside for results. It says and thinks things like: "why do I have to work more hours?" "I wish my boss would give me a raise," "I want more benefits," "I need more vacation time," "I don't like my job," "I wish my boss_________," you fill in the blanks!

This mentality usually looks on the outside of themselves for change and results! It does not see or feel that it has control to change the situation! With the job mentality in sales, your results will be far and few in between. This person won't take the necessary effort required to win at any profession. They show up late whether it's physically or mentally. They leave early whether it's physically or mentally. Oh and by the way someone can always be on time physically and hardly ever be there mentally.

Most jobs have this as a standard, you show up, go through the motions and you get paid! That's a job mentality! But that's not a mindset that will help you succeed in sales! So let's talk about the mindset that's required to be successful as a sales professional! Where the job mentality looks outside, the ownership mentality looks inside! They take full responsibility for their results, implementing any changes necessary to bring better and better results! They show up physically and mentally! They plan their work and work their plan!

They expect to be successful and they are! Looking at these statements one might say the job mentality can't think that way because they are not in control of their activity, but let me assure you they are! If a person has an ownership mentality they usually get to work early, or on time at the least! They show up ready to work with a good attitude that you can see and feel! The CEO of a company will just about always have an ownership mentality and many don't even own the company. The CEO is usually the highest paid employee in the company because they take full responsibility for the results of the company and if the company is not successful they are usually the first to get the blame. And this is the key to their success: their willingness to be responsible without making any excuses!

It's not about the job, it's more about who they are and how they do what they do! They have a standard that they must live up to, irrespective of the business they're working at (someone else's business or their own!) Have you ever heard the statement, *"How you do anything is how you do everything."* This statement refers to habits! Habits are what we create through our thoughts and actions! We first create our habits then our habits create us! Habits are so strong that it's said that we eventually become slaves to them. They master us in every situation, conversation, and activity! And if they go unchecked or unchanged they eventually run us to heaven or to hell on earth!

Think about it, if a person creates a habit of eating healthy and exercising because they do it regularly, eventually it becomes a habit. What benefits can they usually expect? More energy, better sleep, more mental clarity, less physical pain due to aging, and so on and so on! But isn't the reverse true for the person who knowingly or unknowingly creates a habit of eating poorly and not working out! They will most likely have less energy, restless sleep, less mental clarity, more aches and pain, and possibly health conditions common to unhealthy habits! So what habits have you created that will help you succeed selling life insurance? And what habits do you need to change in order to succeed?

Awareness is the first step to change any bad habits that you have. You must first acknowledge the habit and focus on creating its opposite. "The universe abhors a vacuum" that means if you remove something, something else will eventually take its place. So it's important to not only focus on stopping a habit but also on creating its opposite and taking the necessary steps needed to create that new habit.

So let's say for instance you have a habit of starting late. Well you can't focus on not starting late so you have to replace that habit with a new habit of starting early. In order to start this new habit, the key is to just begin and the more you feed this new habit the stronger it gets! It's just like any muscle that you decide to target and to increase. However weak it is in the beginning, the more you exercise it the more you learn about it; and the more you take action to change it the stronger it will become! And that's how you create all the habits you need to be successful!

SET YOURSELF UP TO WIN

So what does success look like for you? What's the goal, result or change that once you achieve will make you feel like you've won? Setting yourself up to win means you know what a win looks like before you start. Zig Ziglar says, *you are either a wandering generality or a meaningful specific.* That means you are either very vague about what you want and Zig says being casual about your goals, results or the change you want in your life will make you a casualty! So you have to be specific, a meaningful specific. You have to know exactly what you want before you start, or if you have already started without knowing what you want then it's time to go back to the drawing board.

Whether you're just getting started in this industry or you have been at it a while, it's never too late or too early to set yourself up to win. There are three stages that you will need to work through in order to set yourself up to win, but before we go to Stage One you have to get clear and specific about what you want.

I started this chapter asking you what success looks like for you? What's the goal, result or change that once you achieve will make you feel like you've won? When I started I had 2 simple very specific goals: *to replace my income,* and *control my time.* I was making around $30,000 a year at the time and working 8am-5pm 5 days a week. The key here is to know what you want and what that looks like to you! This is so important because you can't hit a target you can't see! So for your benefit take the time here to write down what you want out of this industry, both in the short-term and long-term. The long-term can be tricky because you may not know what's possible for you just yet. But the short-term should be very simple to figure out. It's probably the first thing you thought about when this opportunity was presented to you. So with that in mind let's continue.

The three-stage process of setting yourself up to win begins with a process called "Get Ready" then "Fire" and ends with "Aim!" But because success is more of a journey and not just a destination, I recommend you use this process to reach higher and higher levels of success.

I'm sure you've heard the saying "Get Ready, Aim and Fire." This phrase is commonly used in the context of armed service men doing drills over and over again. Our process of setting yourself up to win rearranges the steps to make it more beneficial for goal achievement.

Now let's get to it already…

"Get Ready" means gathering all the necessary materials, training, and equipment. It's learning the

basics and practicing them over and over again until you are confident you can do them. This is the stage where you plan your work, set your schedule, and commit to the outcome you have chosen!

Let me tell you what that looked like for me when I got started long ago. After I passed my test and contacted Ryan, he invited me to my first meeting with the agency. Here he walked me through signing up with a few insurance companies I would use when helping homeowners. He gave me some sales materials so I could learn about the product. He also gave me a sales script to read and an audio cassette to listen too so I could practice what to say when I called the leads. The next day he took me on a ride along with him so I could actually see how it all worked together.

Then I immediately began to listen to the cassette and practice over and over again—on how to make a phone call and do a presentation. I must have listened to that cassette tape for 12 hours memorizing every word and practicing it out loud over and over. This is what getting ready is all about: practice and preparation! A few days after the ride along Ryan contacted me to check in on my progress and I told him everything I was doing. He then said he had some leads in my area he wasn't able to get too so I could have them if I wanted. I agreed and the next day I started making calls, which leads me to the next stage in the process *"Fire"*.

"Fire" is all about action! It's about working the plan consistently and with expectation. When you're new it's important to stay close to your mentor/sponsor so you know how long to stay in this stage. The key here is to just do it! And you must do enough activity in this stage so you have enough information to see if any changes or adjustments need to be made. The "Fire" stage should be a release!

Look at it this way, it's you actually taking physical steps toward your goals, results, and the change you want to bring into your life! Understand that every action you take will produce something—good or bad something got produced. The key here is to work, work, work, and work some more! Your mentor/sponsor should have given you some targets to hit that will help you reach your goals and this is the stage to work those numbers.

Once you've done enough activity let's say at least a months' worth now, it's time to move into the *"Aim"* phase. *"Aim"* is all about looking at the results and making adjustments where needed. This leads me to a very important point; track everything during the "Fire" phase! You should have an activity sheet all through the "Fire" phase to accurately track your activity daily. Every dial, contact made, appointment set, lead closed out, presentation made, sale completed, or no sale made on the presentation needs to recorded.

Keeping an accurate record of your sales activity is so important and absolutely crucial to your success for several reasons. First and foremost you can't fix a problem unless you know what the problem is. Recording all your activity will show you areas that need improvement or things that need adjusted. One example would be if your mentor/sponsor says you should average 1 sale for every 3 presentations and you've done 6 presentations without a sale you could start to think there's a problem. But if you sell your next 3 and now you're 3 sales for 9 presentations you're right where you need to be. But if you don't keep accurate records you won't be able to see inside your business in order to make necessary adjustments when needed.

Also keeping records will help you improve your sales efforts by showing you what activity creates the greatest success. Let me give you an example of how keeping records helped me to see exactly how much I made every time I scheduled a sales appointment. Recently I looked at my records over three months and I noticed that for every appointment I made there was a certain number of sales that came out of the appointments. I then looked at the commissions I earned over this period of time and I did an average of what I got paid in commission for every appointment that got set. So with this information I was able to see exactly how much I earn in commission for every appointment that got scheduled whether I did a presentation on that appointment or not.

As you can see this can be extremely helpful information and encourage a newer agent to schedule more appointments once they realize every appointment they schedule eventually turns into income, no matter the outcome.

It's like a baseball player that goes up to bat. He swings at every pitch but only hits an average of 3 out of 10! Unless he swings at 10 pitches he won't hit 3. That's what an appointment is in this example. It's a swing and the hit is the sale, but you can't have one without the other so as you can see *"Get Ready" "Fire"* and then *"Aim"* will give you the insight to plan and prepare. Then work towards your goal, result, and the outcome you want. And once you've done enough activity, go back to the drawing board and fix whatever needs fixing. Finally, you set a new goal and start the process all over again because this is how you reach higher and higher levels of success. Constantly going through these three stages will give you a complete understanding of what you need to do to bring the result you want into your business.

LEARN MORE ABOUT PEOPLE

THAN PRODUCTS

Your success in this profession is directly tied to people. Your understanding of them and your ability to work with them and influence them to buy is the key to your success in this industry! You don't sell life insurance...no, no, no! You sell people on their need for life insurance and you give them the pleasure of doing business with you!

Understanding the above statement is so important so I'm going to repeat it!

"You don't sell life insurance...no, no, no! You sell people on their need for life insurance and you give them the pleasure of doing business with you."

Because you offer services to people, in order to be successful you must learn more about them, what motivates them, and how to work with them successfully. This is the difference between being successful in this industry or not!

Understanding people begins with understanding what motivates them. People are motivated by two things: *pleasure* and *pain*! They are either seeking pleasure or trying to avoid pain! Think about how this resonates with your own life. What's the last big decision you made? Was it motivated by you seeking a better life? Wanting more control of your future? Wanting your family to have more opportunities than they do now? That's seeking pleasure! Or was it motivated by the fear of loss? Not wanting your family to go without? The fear of losing what you have worked hard for? The fear you won't be seen as who you know yourself to be? These questions represent avoiding pain! These two motivators can be seen in every decision we all make if we take the time and look for them!

"How to Win Friends & Influence People" by Dale Carnegie is the best book by far I have read over the years on understanding people and how to influence them! I have read the hardcopy several times and listened to the audiobook over 20 times throughout the years! The book was first published back in 1936 a long time ago but its principles are timeless! If you were serious about being successful in this industry, my advice would be to make "How to Win Friends and Influence People" a yearly read!

I was first introduced to this book while I was reading a book called "How I raised myself from Failure to Success in Selling" by Frank Bettger (another great book to read by the way!) I was stagnant in my sales and actively looking for resources to improve my results! As I read "How I raised myself from Failure to Success in Selling" he talked so highly about Dale Carnegie and his book so I read it next! These two books helped me tremendously and I still refer back to them just about every year!

In the chapter, Ethical Persuasion, I will go into detail about how to use pleasure and pain while working with people to motivate them ethically to do what's best for them and their family! But for now let's talk a little more about why it's in your best interest to learn more about people than your insurance products!

Think about it this way, toilet paper sells itself! You don't see sales people going out selling toilet paper do you? No! Why? Because it's a product that sells itself! We all need it and we understand what it does! We are also motivated by the fear of what could happen if we run out, right? I'll go ahead and take a leap of faith by saying toilet paper rolls are probably in abundance in your home right now and if not I'm sure they will be soon!

Life insurance on the other hand has been proven to be a product not found in over 30% of the households in the US Today and over half of US households that have Life Insurance are said to be underinsured-LIMRA Feb 2020.

Why is that? Why do so many households either lack the necessary amount of life insurance to take care of their family or go without a policy altogether? Think about this for a moment. Life insurance has never been so easy to purchase. You can't watch TV long enough without seeing a commercial to buy a policy and we are constantly being bombarded with ads in newspapers, online and radio to *call* or *click* to buy a policy. So why do so many people go without life insurance or know they don't have enough?

Because we haven't sold it to them yet! Unlike toilet paper, in most cases, life insurance must be sold! Most people know they need it and a good percentage of them have the intention to buy more real soon so why don't they just call or click and do it? Procrastination for one reason or another is the answer here and their reason for not clicking or calling goes on and on! But here is where our opportunity is found, because if people didn't procrastinate there would be no opportunity for life insurance sales agents. Nope. Not at all! The industry would only need people to answer questions, make suggestions, and complete applications! At least until they replace all of them with artificial intelligence.

In my opinion procrastination is the number one reason our opportunity exists! So it's what we get paid to help people through, around, over, and under! Because of this understanding, motivating people will be the key to your success in selling life insurance. Have you ever heard of Pareto Law, also known as the 80–20 rule? It states that 80% of the result is produced by 20% of the effort! This principle has been proven to be true over and over again! 20% of people make 80% of the money in every industry. 20% of your clients will be responsible for 80% of your commissions and on and on!

One way to use this rule to help you succeed in this industry is to focus 80% of your time on the 20% of the things that pay you the most! We will discuss this more in the chapters ahead but for the purposes of this chapter, use 80% of your study time to understanding people and 20% to understanding your company's product! This will allow you to help more people which in turn will dramatically increase your sales!

Core principles you must understand & Apply in order to Sell Successfully

Selling is all about influencing people to act and in order to influence them you must understand them. There are three core principles that can help you work with anyone, anywhere, and at any time.

The first principle is: "People don't care how much you know until they know how much you care!" This principle lies at the door of influence and the heart of persuasion. This principle looks at the why of the situation and the motive behind it. When someone feels that you genuinely care about them, what happens to them, and their situation in general, an unspoken connection will manifest. It's that teacher that loves her students so much that influences the worst kid in the school to become better! The student that's always in trouble, acting out and fighting usually doesn't feel like anyone cares. Then that special teacher comes along and with interest and involvement that teacher influences the worst student in a way that no one has been able to. What magic does that teacher hold? What power does he or she wield? Why were they able to do what no other teacher could? It's simple: they cared and were able to get that student to see that they did!

When someone believes that you care about them, their situation and what happens to them, you immediately build trust! And trust is the greatest currency when working with people! If you have enough of it, you can do just about anything! If you don't there is nothing you can do. The key here comes down to why you're doing this in the first place and whether you really care? If your why has purpose and meaning it will translate! People will see, hear and feel that you really do care about them then and only then will they care to listen to you!

Don't cheat the market here and cheat yourself! We all have bills and our own financial interest of course, but this principle goes so much deeper. It looks into the heart and shows what's really there! All this principle requires of you is investing some time with your *why* and understanding it. I believe we all care but those who feel it and make others feel it too think about it often. They meditate on it and it shows up in their conversations. It becomes a passion, a mission; something bigger than themselves and that's where influence is created! This only works when it's real! So make it real! Have you felt the pain of any family members not having or not having enough life insurance? Why do you believe in life insurance in the first place?

Knowing the answer to these questions will put you in the right frame of mind and help you connect with your client in a way that will help you to work with them.

The next principle is: "People like to do business with people that they trust!" Remember trust is the currency of getting things done when working with people. I remember years ago when I was a kid and my family went to Cedar Point. Back then I wasn't tall enough to get on the rides, however my older sister and brothers were able to get on so I had to stand and watch while they rode the rides I desperately wanted to ride as well! Without trust a relationship just won't go anywhere because one or both parties won't get on! You see trust is like the entry point to the rides I wasn't tall enough to get on. It's the minimum requirement to proceed. And the key to building trust is to be likable. People like people who are like them, who listen to them, and who have a pleasing personality. All of these will help people to like you and thereby be willing to do business with you.

Think about some people you have done business with in the past and why you chose them. What about them stood out? Was it the timing or a connection? I would venture to say it was a little or a lot of both. When I say people like people who are like them I mean *tone* and *demeanor*. Both can be slightly matched to make your prospect more comfortable with you. The key here is to be yourself but if you're meeting with someone who's softly-spoken and you're naturally loud, bring it down a few levels to make them feel more comfortable. If you're naturally low and quiet but you're meeting with someone who's loud, bring it up a bit! Match them but don't copy! Be yourself but get on their level is what I saying here.

People like people who listen to them. Listening is an art well forgotten in our day and age. People nowadays usually listen without trying to understand. They are usually thinking of their response rather than trying to understand what the other person is saying and why they are saying it. So the key here is to listen to understand! Get inside the person's head and then you can easily access their heart! And in the heart is where influence begins. You can then help them help themselves by showing them themselves and what life could look like if they don't act now. This then leads me to the final principal of the 3: "People love to buy but they hate to be sold."

This is all about showing them what they said and why they said it! It's not about you and what you think they should do, it's about them and what they said they want! Remember you don't sell life insurance! You sell people on their need for life insurance! A need that they have told you is important to them! Then you give them the benefits of buying it through you. Allowing someone to buy is all about removing the obstacles out of their way and letting them choose what's best for them because only they know what's best for them! People love to buy because buying says they made the decision! They decided to act! They own it! People hate to be sold because it was pushed on them! It was forced! Our responsibility isn't to push our prospects into anything or force them to do anything! Our responsibility is to simply remove any and all obstacles so they can do what's best for themselves and their family! And when they know we care, and they like us as well they will choose to do business with us and enjoy it!

I could literally write a book about these three principles and maybe I will, but for now I wanted to introduce you to them so you can see what really motivates your prospects and why they will choose

you when you understand them.

ETHICAL PERSUASION & PRESENTATION POWER

So let's put something together and see a compounding effect! Let's say you actually take some time and invest into becoming a professional! You learn more about people than your products, and you become a student of them! Let's say over time you get a great grasp of the three core principles and you begin to apply them to your sales presentation. You also start to understand how and when to use them to motivate your prospects to make a decision!

Understand that this is a unique skill that I assure you will put you in the 20% of top income earners in our industry when you apply it regularly. And that's why ethical persuasion needs to be the driver of this high-powered machine you now own! You see a skill is a tool—something that allows you to get a job done. It makes the users' job easier and gives them more leverage to accomplish the task. In the right hands a tool can be used to create masterpieces but in the wrong hands that tool can be used for destruction.

Ethical persuasion is all about leaving your prospect better than you found them. It's the financial order to do no harm! Unfortunately, I've seen insurance agents put their needs and desires for a quick pay day over what's best for the client too many times. I've sat down with prospects who were told lies just so the agent could replace a good policy with one of lesser value. It's a real problem that affects our industry as a whole because the whole is merely a sum of its parts! So I encourage you to use this tool to only do good! I ask that you do what's best for the client and Do No Harm! I ask that you use this skill to help them as if they were your family that you love and adore because someone loves them like you do your family.

Remember we reap what we sow and I truly believe karma is undefeated so only do what you truly believe to be Right!

Okay so now that we have gotten that out of the way, let's talk a little about presentation power! I believe a successful presentation is made up of several parts and the first is the *warm up*. The warm up consist of you taking some time to get to know the prospect and showing you care about them and their situation. This is best done through a process called FORM which is a series of questions that when used properly allows you to connect with the prospect. Remember core principle number 1 "People don't care how much you know until they know how much you care" so FORM will allow you to show them that you care before you try to influence them. FORM is an acronym that stands for **F**amily, **O**ccupation, **R**ecreation, and **M**essage.

Family is where we talk to them about their kids and relatives. It's where you try to get a picture of what's going on inside their life. Occupation is where you talk to them about their job—what they do, how they do it, how long they've done it, whether they like it or not, what they enjoy about it and so on. This will give you an idea of their personality and what's important to them. Recreation goes further and talks to them about what they enjoy doing personally to get an even clearer picture of who they are. And finally is the message where you begin to interject the conversation with your purpose for being there. It's where you begin to put together how you can help them accomplish their needs and desires through your product. FORM is so important because if gives you the framework to make suggestions and recommendations.

Next is establishing credibility. It's where you tell them a little about who you are and why you do what you do. Let them see you and open up here! Honesty is the best policy! If you're new use it and if you've been doing this for years use that! Either one can be positioned as an asset! Let's say you're brand new and it's one of your first sales appointments. During this phase of the presentation you can simply say, "Mr & Mrs Smith, I'm brand new to this amazing industry! I recently received my license a few (....) ago and this gives me a unique advantage and prospective because the concepts and information I'll be sharing with you I've seen help so many through the recent training and development program that I've recently passed! Instead of being just another client to someone doing this for years and years, you folks will be important to me because you're my first! Isn't that great Mr & Mrs Smith..."

You see, if you position something the right way, anything you think is a liability can be positioned as an asset!

After credibility comes then the carrier overview! This is where you talk about the company you are about to present and why they stand head and shoulders above the rest of the options out there.

Then it's time for the product overview. The product overview should explain the key points to the product: the pleasure the owners receive and the pain it insures won't happen. Remember pleasure and pain? Remember people only take action to get pleasure or avoid pain. But know this; people will move faster to avoid pain than to acquire pleasure; so in most cases your presentation should be worded with this in mind!

Finally, is the close! This is where you present the options and you ask for a decision! Over the years you would not believe how many agents I've seen not ask the prospect for a decision! Yes, it's okay to ask for a decision; absolutely!!! But once you do the next key is to be quiet because whoever talks first just bought! Always remember that when you ask a closing question don't say another word! You must allow the prospect to buy! Remember people Love to Buy but they Hate to be Sold! So let them buy and don't say another word until they do!!! This type of presentation can be used to successfully sell any product within our industry to a qualified prospect with a need. We will talk about leads and qualified prospects in the next chapter but for now let's put the icing on this cake.

Last but not least is Enthusiasm! Enthusiasm is so important to your presentation I literally could write an entire chapter or even a book about enthusiasm and how important it is to any presentation. It's enthusiasm that gives your **Presentation Power**! With enthusiasm a bad presentation can be a successful one and without it no presentation is good enough. Enthusiasm is the excitement, the certainty, and the passion you have for the product. It presents the product in a way that connects your prospect to the product and gives them the ability to see how and why they need it in the first place.

Enthusiasm literally will make you more sales than an amazing presentation ever could. Because without enthusiasm a presentation has no life; without enthusiasm a presentation has no feeling. It's like a great recipe without the seasoning—it's bland. So do yourselves a favor and get excited, be passionate about the information you're presenting, and say it in a way that makes you feel what you're doing is important because enthusiasm starts on the inside of you and is expressed outward to them and when you have it they automatically will.

So you must have it first. You must get excited about the information you're sharing and how it will provide value to them and their family for years and years to come. Enthusiasm is what gives your **Presentation Power!!!**

LEADS, LEADS, AND MORE LEADS

Leads are the lifeblood of business! Whether it's Real Estate, retail, manufacturing, or any other one of the industries that supports the economy, every industry has a sales/marketing department and leads are a huge part of what's needed for every business to be successful. I've always said over the years that a lead is only as good as the agent working it! A great agent can turn a bad lead into a treasure and a bad agent can turn a good lead into trash!

A lead is just an opportunity to present your case. It gives you a chance to win the prospect to your way of thinking. As long as the lead is qualified it doesn't matter if it's direct mail, Internet, telemarketing, or door-to-door survey. A lead is not a sale! It's an opportunity! That's why it's so important for you to become a professional, for you to understand people and how to influence them! That's the key—not the lead!

So what's the difference between qualified and non-qualified, and which one should you use becomes the question. In my opinion a non-qualified lead is more of a general interest and not a specific need. It's a lead that offers something in order for the prospect to take a look. One example of this lead is a lead I've seen over the years offering a $5 Walmart card to return the form for information about life insurance. I've seen agents have great success with these leads and love them. I've also seen agents fail to succeed with these leads and hate them.

It's definitely a general lead but it gets you in the door and for a great agent that's all they need! Just a way in and they'll make it happen! I've always said if it's a sale to be made I'll make it! That's the mindset of a winning agent. And they walk in that belief and back it with action!

A non-qualified lead should be cheaper than a qualified lead because they are easier to acquire. A qualified lead will cost more per lead because they are harder to acquire.

One example of a qualified lead would be a mortgage protection lead. They are specific because they are only sent out to individuals who have recently refinanced a mortgage or purchased a home. That's specific, and you only call on the leads that return the request for information and by that they have just indicated their interest by returning the form. You can even funnel this process down further and have someone else call these leads to ask a series of questions to qualify them even more. But for now I'd rather talk to you about something rarely talked about and often overlooked in our industry!

I would like to talk to you about the return on your investment! You see that's the key when it comes to working leads. How much is the return on your investment and how quick can you recoup your investment?

This brings me back to tracking everything you do so you can see inside your business and know what's working well for you and what's not. If you're working multiple lead types, you should track your results on each and every lead type so you can see where your investment is best made.

Another thing I've seen over the years is in order to have success you must invest time and money! Every sale will require a combination of both. Let's say you track your results for a while and you see that you're having more success with one lead over another but that lead costs three times as much as the other lead. You may initially think that this lead has a greater investment cost but let's look closer. Let's say your recently responded mortgage protection lead has a cost of $45 per lead. As I write this chapter that's the average cost in the open market as of now. Let's also say you can purchase a telemarketing mortgage protection lead for $15 each. So the lead response by mail is more of an initial investment. But after time of working both leads you see that your cost per sale is $135 for the mail-responded mortgage protection lead because you sell 1 out of every 3 leads you work. And after working the telemarketing lead for a while you see your cost per sale is $150 because you sell 1 out of every 10 leads that you work.

By understanding your cost per sale you can literally write your own paycheck and decide exactly how much you want to make by investing what you need to in order to achieve the results you desire.

This information is extremely important because it tells you a few things. First it tells you that your cost per sale is lower with the mail-responded leads and it also tells you that your time is better invested with the mail-responded leads as well, because you don't have to work as many leads in order to get to your result. This information over the long run will greatly impact your business and how profitable you are.

Time is your greatest commodity and it's non-renewable! You only get so much on a daily basis to work your business so you absolutely must invest it wisely! When it comes to leads my advice is to focus on your cost per sale and your time per sale as well. But in my opinion put the greater value on your time because that is a non-renewable resource. If you have access to a lead that costs more per sale but gives you the same results as some of your other leads but in 1/3 of the time, that might be the better choice. Obviously there are other things to consider and your situation will help you make that choice.

The key here is to always watch these numbers and do what you can to improve them. Looking into your business is just as important as working it; or sometimes even more important when it comes to you being profitable. So for now let's move to chapter number 8.

How to handle objections successfully

The first thing to understand about an objection is that it's not a bad thing! An objection is just a request for more information. There is something that your prospect needs before they feel good about moving forward. The key here is to always remember what you're there to do. Your number one job is to help them make a decision! Now that decision won't always lead to them buying a policy because maybe that's not what's in their best interest at the time. But it usually will be. Your presentation should be designed to eliminate the most common objections. So I'll invest our time together focusing on the one you will probably get the most, which is "let me think about it," or "I'll get back to you and let you know."

This objection has caused more salesmen to leave their industry than any other and it will put you right out of business if you can't overcome it on a daily basis. This objection within itself doesn't give you enough information to successfully handle it and unfortunately that's what most salespeople try to do. They proceed with trying to overcome this objection without first knowing why the prospect said it in the first place.

In all my years of selling I've noticed that this objection is more of a smokescreen than something the prospect will actually do. It's usually their way of getting you out the door so they don't have to plainly tell you they can't afford the options you have shown them. So that's where I usually start if and when I hear the "Lamar that looks great but give us some time to think about it and we'll let you know." Think of it this way: if we're best friends you still probably wouldn't want to confide in me that you can't afford the options I'm showing you for a policy to protect your family. So instead of telling this to a semi-stranger, your prospect will just try to put you off thereby putting off the decision altogether. If you've gotten this far into the process and presentation, you owe it to them and yourself to help them get to the real issue so you can work with them to overcome it!

In most of my presentations I bring up this objection and handle it before the prospect has a chance too. So before I show them the options I'll usually say something like this:

"John and Susie, before we go over the options for your coverage I would like to make you a quick promise. I promise you that I will do everything in my ability to help you folks find a plan that not only fits your needs but also fits your budget or suit would you feel comfortable investing into this type of protection on a monthly basis. Now in order for me to keep that promise I need you folks to make me a promise as well. And that promise is that once I show you these initial options you won't look at them and look at each other, then look back at me and tell me you want to think about it. And it's for your benefit that I'm asking you not to say that. Because usually if I hear that from my clients it's because they don't understand some information that I've presented or the monthly options aren't quite where they want them to be.

So if there's anything you don't understand please just ask because that's what I'm here for. And if any of the options you like aren't where you need them to be on a monthly basis, just let me know and I'll show you how we can make some adjustments to get them more to where you need them to be. So John and Susie, does that sound fair to you?"

The key here is to make sure they understand you're here to help. You're on their team! You can change the type of product, lower the coverage amount, or even shorten the term. You can do a lot of different things to help them afford the coverage so they know their family is protected!

This again is another topic I can cover a whole book on but for now the key to remember is that no matter what the objection is you have to get to the real issue. You must find the real reason the objection has come up in the first place. Don't assume you know and don't try to close them until you do!

DEALING WITH THE UPS & DOWNS

Here's the thing, no matter how great your system is or how great you are at working it, you will be tested emotionally and psychologically by this business. Over the last 18 years I've seen people come and go that seem to have all the necessary ingredients to win, but were obviously missing the one that mattered the most—which is understanding how to deal with the ups and downs of the business.

Because you are in a business that deals with people, detriments like commissions, chargebacks, cancellations, no show appointments, denials, and many more frustrating situations can, and will, put you out of this business if you don't look at them from the right perspective; thereby removing all the wonderful advantages of being a part of this industry which include but are not limited to *commissions, renewals, approvals, company-sponsored trips, awards, time freedom,* along with meeting new and wonderful people.

Dealing with the ups and downs start with being aware that for everything that's good about this business, its opposite also exist. It's you understanding that no matter what's going on you hold the power through your thoughts and actions to change the situation, or go create a new and better one.

No opportunity is perfect. Every opportunity on one hand has blessings, the things we want; and curses on other hand, the things we don't want! The key here is to focus on what you want and to constantly work towards it. And when those trials and tribulations come as they inevitably will, you must learn to use them as fuel to go further, work harder, and work smarter!

Look at it this way. If you're working with the right mindset and a positive attitude every action you take toward your desired result will produce something. That something may be exactly what you want or not so much, but if you understand the law of averages which we will discuss in the next chapter then you know it's just a matter of time before you get to your desired result! Dealing with the downs of this business presents you with a unique opportunity to show yourself what you're made of! It gives you the evidence that you belong here and no matter what life throws your way, you can and will overcome it!

Dealing with the ups of this business also presents you with a unique opportunity to show yourself that you are thankful for the success you have created through your thoughts and actions but at the same time you're not too full of yourself! It's all about balance and consistency!

Don't allow your emotions to rule you. You must rule over them! Whether things are going better than you could have ever imagined or worse than you ever expected, you're responsible! I know that's a tough pill to swallow during the down times but it's the one that will put you back in control of your business and the outcome you want! When things are going amazingly well as they inevitably will, you have to continue the thoughts and actions that resulted in that success if you want it to continue! This is obviously easier to do than pulling yourself out of a slump so let's focus our time and attention there. But the last thing I'll say on handling the ups of this business is: Pride comes before a fall! Be humble, grateful, and thankful always. Don't ever let your success go to your head, keep it in your heart by having an attitude of gratitude!

Okay! So now let's finish up with dealing with the downs. The key with dealing with the downs of this business is just working through them! You have to work with a positive mental attitude and an expectation of success. The worst thing you can do is to pull back and let up! You have to increase your activity because that is what will lead you back to the upswing. This is a time that it becomes hard to do so but if you're serious about reaching your goals, dreams and desires, this is the test you must pass.

Just about every time I miss a sale, I remind myself that even Jesus didn't get everybody and how can I expect to be better than Jesus. This has always reminded me to keep going! Because my next one will be my best one and if I stay in the game I'll win!

Another thing I remind myself of if things are happening in the business that I don't want or care for! I'm putting the numbers in my favor because the harder I work the luckier I get!

Hopefully this helps you to discipline your disappointments and help you keep the right perspective at all times. A perspective that will help you to continue to do the necessary actions required to win and succeed! Now let's talk a little about the three keys to winning in sales.

The 3 Keys to winning in sales (Activity, Consistency & Persistence)

Success in sales is not some unattainable faraway place that only the fortunate few can visit and stay. No! It's a place you have to pay the cost to visit each and every day! And these three keys will make sure there's always room for you!

So let's look at them one by one and see what happens when we use all three!

Activity is playing the numbers and expecting to win! It's understanding the Law of Averages and using it to win in sales. The Law of Averages states that if you do something long enough a ratio will appear and once a ratio starts they tend to continue!

In baseball we call it batting average. A batter steps up to the plate and hits 3 out of 10; that means he has 300% for his batting average! That also means he's out 7 times out of 10! In baseball you make over 4 million dollars per year if you're out 7 out of 10 because you bat a 300%. It's similar in sales! If you can close 30% of your leads which is an average of 3 out of 10 you can write your own paycheck selling life insurance!

The Law of Averages can be increased. A brand new agent may start out averaging sales on 1 out of every 10 leads because they're new and don't have a grasp of the entire sales process or how to handle objections. With time, experience and training that agent can see their close rate increase from 1 out of 10 to 2 out of 10 and then 3 out of 10. 3 out of 10 is sufficient to help you reach the top 20% of income earners in this business and the key to getting there is to work the numbers.

The more you realize it's just a numbers game, the more success you can have and maintain. Every part of the sales process is all about numbers and working them to achieve your desired results! The number of leads you receive weekly will determine how many prospects you contact. How many prospects you contact will determine how many appointments you set weekly. How many appointments you set weekly will determine how many prospects you actually see. And finally how many prospects you actually see will determine how many sales you make that week.

Each number will be less than its predecessor and it's these numbers that presents you the greatest opportunity in this business. Let's say you get 10 qualified leads per week and out of the 10 leads you contact 8. Out of the 8 contacted (out of the previous

10) you set sales appointments with 5 of them. You show up on time to each of the 5 to find out that only 4 of them are home at the appointed time. You do a great presentation for each of the 4 and 3 of them decide to purchase your product! Let's also assume you make on average $700 in commissions for each sale paying you $2,100 for that week. Not bad, right? Well let's also say you want to double your pay so instead of getting 10 qualified leads per week you increase your order to 20 leads. By understanding your averages and using the Law of Averages you can expect to make $4,200 in commissions from those 20 leads! Now there are other factors that can come into play here that can help you or hurt you so let's discuss the next key to winning in sales which is Consistency.

Consistency is all about staying sharp and putting your best effort into each and every lead, phone call, and sales presentation. Consistency is needed to get winning results! Imagine if a professional baseball player stopped swinging his bat with expectation and power! Imagine if he went to the plate and thought I'll just swing at each one…who cares if I hit it or not! He definitely will hit one from time to time but his results will be greatly diminished. It's no different from us in sales! You have to show up each and every time if you want to win! You may not know where your next sale will come from but you have to swing with expectation at each and every lead in order to find it!

Consistency is a key because without it your results will be far less than they could be with it!

Finally, we come to persistence! Persistence is all about staying in the game long enough so you can win! Persistence is all about following through. It's the sales agent that keeps going, going and going because they know success is out there and they won't stop until they reach it! Persistence is what separates the beginner from the professional! The beginner may understand and work the Law of Averages! They may also be consistent in their efforts dealing with each and every lead. But persistence is the test every beginner must pass to become a professional and keep passing in order to stay one!

In business as in life we seldom have to be told, but we frequently need to be reminded of what's important! These three keys seem so simple and they are but let's not confuse simple with easy! Life will always be waiting to get in your way and make it inconvenient for you to do your activity or for you to be consistent with each and every lead. So you will have to persist if you want to stay in the game and win!

When you put these three keys into your business and work them regularly you can and will achieve any goal you are willing to work for in this business. Now let's move on to the final chapter to learn how to grow your income.

YOUR INCOME CAN ONLY GROW TO THE EXTENT THAT YOU DO

Have you ever heard the statement: "Your income can only grow to the extent that you do"? This statement refers to your personal growth and how your income is tied directly to it! Your personal growth deals with your mindset, thoughts, and actions. It's what you believe is possible for you and your perspective on life. It's how you see the world and respond to it. Growing your income is not an outside job of what you do or don't do. It's an inside job of what you expect and what you will or won't accept. The best way to become a millionaire isn't having a million dollars in the bank; it's becoming a millionaire on the inside through growing yourself personally and professionally. Then attracting a million dollars through your actions because of who you are and what you believe is possible for you!

We hear story after story of people who have been blessed with sudden windfalls of money beyond their wildest dreams only to end up with nothing to show for it in the end.

We also see stories of people who have started with nothing amass great wealth and abundance. These two types of people are only separated by growth and development. One took the time to work on themselves. They learned and they grew! They developed themselves whether it was by reading, relationships, or a combination of both. They did the work to grow from the inside out. The other received a windfall but because they didn't have the necessary development to keep it and grow it they eventually lost it!

So let's be clear about this! Your income is more of a reflection of who you are and what you believe is possible for you than a fact predetermined by society. It's something that you can grow and develop like a muscle or your vocabulary through trial and effort.

The best way I've found to grow myself personally and professionally is by establishing consistent routines that allow me to work on myself consciously and unconsciously. I work out regularly, usually 3-4 times per week not because I like it but because I know it's necessary if I want to have the available energy needed to work hard and persist! I listen to motivational messages, sales training, and leadership development while driving. I read books on the same topics so I can constantly sharpen my awareness and become a better version of myself which will always attract better results! I attend workshops on personal and professional development inside this industry and others that align with my vision for the future I want to create for myself and my family. Successful people don't like to do the things unsuccessful people don't like to do either, but the difference is they do them anyway because they know it's the price you must pay to achieve the success.

I just want to add that by doing the things you don't like to do but you know will help you achieve what you want to achieve, you will probably start to love those things that you, at one time or another, didn't like.

And doing these things has grown my income and it will grow yours too! You see we don't get in life what we want, we get in life what we are! So who are you? A more important question is who do you want to be and are you willing to do the work on yourself to become it? No one was born a finished masterpiece! We all have to become who we are and that takes time, energy and effort! Your best days are always ahead of you!

There is no limit to your potential and what you can accomplish if you're willing to work on yourself! It's your responsibility! It's your investment in this area that will eventually make the greatest return in this business and any other ventures you pursue! So with that being said thanks for your time and investment in reading this book! It absolutely shows you're on the right track to achieve any and all of your goals, dreams, and desires. You have already done what 80% of this industry refuses to do and if you keep on this path of learning, growing and implementing things that will help you grow, there is no limit to what you can and will achieve. So always remember if you want to grow your income, first, grow yourself!

About The Author

Lamar Skipper is the Owner & Founder of Work Smarter Insurance & Quality Insurance LLC based in Toledo, Ohio. Lamar loves to help agents work smarter so they can leverage their time, energy, and effort while helping more people in less time!

He believes that life insurance is an important key to helping prevent financial and economic hardship and by helping agents to succeed he can help far more families get the coverage they need and want! Connect with Lamar on youtube.com/user/lamarskipper & www.worksmarterinsurance.com